# Eyes Upon the Land

## The Territorial Integrity of Israel:
## A Life-Threatening Concern

BASED ON THE PUBLIC STATEMENTS
AND WRITINGS OF
THE LUBAVITCHER REBBE,
RABBI MENACHEM M. SCHNEERSON

adapted by Rabbi Eliyahu Touger

edited by Uri Kaploun

Published by
**Sichos In English**
788 Eastern Parkway • Brooklyn, New York 11213
718-778-5436

5757 • 1997

# EYES UPON THE LAND

Published and Copyrighted by
**SICHOS IN ENGLISH**
788 Eastern Parkway • Brooklyn, N.Y. 11213
Tel. (718) 778-5436

**ISBN 1-8814-0020-4**

5757 • 1997

# PUBLISHER'S FOREWORD

## AN INTERACTIVE POSSESSION

Our Sages teach[1] that every Jew possesses a portion of *Eretz Yisrael*, the Land of Israel. The converse is also true. The land possesses a portion of every Jew.

For this is[2] "a land which G-d... seeks out; the eyes of G-d are always upon it, from the beginning of the year until the end of the year." And just as G-d seeks out the land, so do we. We gobble up all the news about it. Barely a day passes without the land being in the headlines. And, because the land possesses a portion of every Jew, day after day you and I look in the small print to seek out what's happening.

There is certainly a lot happening. Unfortunately, however, not all of it is positive. Much of our concern for Israel is motivated by apprehension over the fate of the Jews there. Ever since independence and even before, there has been a climate of worry and fear caused by the threats and attacks of its Arab neighbors.

## THERE IS NO MAGIC FORMULA

In recent years, it has become common to think of the solution of the Arab-Israeli conflict in terms of the formula,

---

1. *Responsa of Rabbeinu Meir ben Baruch*, Responsum 536 (in *Otzar HaGeonim* on Tractate *Kiddushin*, sec. 146).
2. *Deuteronomy* 11:12.

"land for peace." Phrasing the question in that manner produces a ready answer, for regardless of our love for the Land of Israel, there is no question that all sacrifices necessary should be made to achieve peace.

But phrasing the question in that manner is not only an oversimplification; it distorts the issues at hand. Why should conceding land be considered a step toward peace? Let us take a look at the history of the last three years. Israel transferred land both to the Palestinians and the Jordanians, and was very near to returning land to the Syrians. Did this bring her any closer to peace?

The tally of deaths stemming from Palestinian terrorism hit record highs. Arafat is still calling for *jihad* (Arabic for a holy war). Relations with Jordan are far less warm than before the peace treaty was signed. And Syria is demanding outright surrender of the Golan as a precondition to talks, or threatening war.

Maybe something was wrong with the premise?

Israelis definitely thought change was necessary. At the recent elections, more than 60% of the country's Jewish inhabitants decided to choose a new prime minister — and this despite the fact that the news media in the country staunchly supported the Labor government, and President Clinton publicly endorsed Shimon Peres.

But changing the faces at the helm is not enough. That became obvious when the prime minister chosen because of a rightist platform went on to follow — with only slight changes — the policies initiated by the previous government.

The difficulties in Israeli-Arab relations stem from problems lying at the core of the issue. Therefore, surface changes in approach will do no more than bring about superficial variations. Only by changing the paradigm as a whole can we hope for lasting improvement.

## A FOCUS ON LIFE

In the pages that follow, we will present a different approach to the issues, one rooted in the principles of our Jewish heritage, yet starkly realistic in its appreciation of what is happening on the ground in and around Israel today.

At its core is concern for life and security. After the Oslo and Hebron agreements, people have eulogized the old dream of a greater Israel. They have heralded these treaties as signs of Israel's willingness to bypass its concern for land and focus on making peace. As we will explain, however, the very reason for our concern for the land is the security it grants us. And it is because basic civilian safety and security are being jeopardized that these recent agreements are so painful to bear.

Any candid observer can see that these agreements are merely buying time — and at an unaffordable price. Concession after concession is being made because "otherwise the Arabs will riot." And this is called "peace."

Before and after the Hebron agreements, the right wing camp inside and outside Israel has been forced to defend itself ideologically time and time again. Hence, in the heat of pressure and oft-repeated arguments, the debater himself can lose sight of his original intent.

For this reason, we have sought to present fundamental principles that lie at the very heart of the issue. Our exposition is based on the public statements of the Lubavitcher Rebbe, beginning from the period directly after the Six-Day War until 1992, when he suffered a stroke that prevented him from speaking. Although the Rebbe's talks and letters date from years ago, their immediate relevance is uncanny. At times, they appear to have been delivered and written just yesterday. The clarity of the Rebbe's words and his penetrating insight enable us to see the situation as it is and recognize our priorities.

Moreover, his words inspire, motivating us to translate them from the abstract into the actual.

## BASING POLICY ON PRINCIPLE

Our exposition is divided into two sections:

Part I, which is theoretical, outlines the fundamental principles which the Rebbe saw as lying at the heart of the Israeli-Arab conflict.

Part II, which is historical, outlines several phases in the Israeli-Arab conflict; the approach taken by the Israeli government; and the suggestions which the Rebbe made at those times. In this section, we have also highlighted the almost prophetic vision which the Rebbe demonstrated with regard to Israel's struggles. For this emphasizes that his approach is not one of theoretical idealism, but one which is in touch with both what can be seen — and what is on the horizon – in Israel today.

To underscore the fundamental principles that motivate the Rebbe's approach we have not quoted his words verbatim, but instead telescoped them, synthesizing points from many different addresses into an organic whole.

We have tried to maintain the integrity of the Rebbe's words by not expanding them beyond the contexts in which they were originally spoken. Thus, although many of the concepts we have outlined obviously relate to the contemporary situation in Israel, we have generally left it to our readers to make the connections.

This approach also serves another purpose. Our intent is not to support any particular party in Israel, but rather to motivate people to take a new and different look at the situation in its entirety. Were we to focus on the immediate issues, our statements might be viewed as rhetoric coming from one side of the political spectrum.

Instead, we appeal to responsible people on every side of that spectrum. Our fundamental point: the importance of the preservation of Jewish life is one that all identify with. We are asking that this principle be given the primacy it deserves, and that it serve as a guiding light to determine the priorities Israel must set for itself.

May the principles we outline lead to peace and security in Israel today, and may they lead to the age when[3] "nation will not lift up sword against nation, nor will they learn war any more."

## IN APPRECIATION

This publication is sponsored by Rabbi Joseph Gutnick, a champion of the security and the integrity of our holy land. He has invested both effort and resources to ensure the fulfillment of the Divine promise:[4] "You will dwell securely in your land; I will provide peace in the land; you will lie down and no one will make you afraid."

Sichos In English

25 Adar I, 5757
[March 4, 1997]

---

3.  *Isaiah* 2:4.
4.  *Leviticus* 26:5-6.

# PART I:

# THE PRINCIPLES UNDERLYING THE ISRAEL-ARAB CONFLICT

## AT THE CORE OF THE ISSUE

"Whoever destroys a Jewish life is considered to have destroyed an entire world. And whoever saves a Jewish life is considered to have saved an entire world."[1]

In Jewish thought, this construct does not serve as merely a theoretical and ethical truth, but as a practical directive. Our heritage is rich in treasured laws and values, but when their application threatens human life, their practice is temporarily suspended.

This concept has resounded within the consciousness of the world at large: the protection of human life has been accepted as the fundamental raison d'être for the existence of governments. As the US Constitution proclaims, the very first purpose of a government is to provide its citizens with "life."

To apply this concept to the present situation in the Land of Israel: Although almost 30 years that have passed since the Six-Day War, and despite efforts by all the world powers, there is no immediate sign of peace. Now if anyone wants to stop treading water and make real progress, he has to put first things first, identify his issue of primary concern and make it the focus of his argument.

The question of primary concern to Israel is obvious: What is the course of action that will protect Jewish — and for that matter, Arab — lives most effectively?

---

1.     Tractate *Sanhedrin* 4:5.

(We mention Jewish lives first. Although all humans are created "in the image of G-d,"[2] and every life must be cherished, the Torah teaches Jews to place Jewish life as the highest priority. And slightly more than 50 years after the world stood idly by as a third of our people were annihilated, no further explanation is necessary. We have learned that if we do not stand up for ourselves, no one else will.[3])

Many Americans live far away from tragedy, and we often view a death as a statistic. We react to a report on a terrorist attack by counting the numbers. "They got three of ours, but we killed four of theirs. So we won." Not only is such an approach callous; it misses the entire point. The question should not be who killed more, but how to prevent killing.

In the pages that follow, we will examine several dimensions of the Arab-Israeli conflict. Over and above all, our focus will be guided by the principle stressed above — the preservation of life.


## WHAT RISKS CAN YOU BE WILLING TO TAKE?

It is hard not to become caught up with the immediacy of an issue. Especially when one is concerned with a subject like peace, there is a natural desire to hastily seek an agreement as soon as possible. Nevertheless, this feeling of immediacy should never be allowed to obscure the priorities involved. If the peace is to last longer than the time it took to hammer out

---

2.  *Genesis* 1:27.
3.  Even when, as in the Iraqi invasion of Kuwait, America did ultimately intervene, that intervention came several months after the invasion, after extensive loss of life and destruction of property. Similarly, in Bosnia, Somalia and Zaire, the world's conscience has been slow in awakening and ineffective in acting. Heaven forbid that what has happened in those countries would ever happen in the Land of Israel.

the agreement, we must make sure that it realistically answers the objectives that we seek.

What does Israel want out of peace? Two fundamental objectives:

(a) that it be secure against attack from the surrounding Arab nations;

(b) that its citizens may rest assured that their lives will not be endangered by terrorist attack.

These objectives are primarily military issues. Therefore it is military experts who should be consulted for the parameters according to which any negotiations should be conducted.

To refer to a parallel: When there is a question of whether the Sabbath laws must be violated to save the life of a patient, the Torah prescribes that one ask an expert — a doctor; more specifically, a doctor in the relevant field.[4] For a heart condition one consults a cardiologist, not a dermatologist.

To return to the analog: There are many dimensions to the Israeli-Arab conflict. Nevertheless, just as when a person has a heart condition, it is the cardiologist whose opinion is given highest priority, since Israel's fundamental concerns are questions of security, it is the opinions of military men and particularly, those trained in the issues at hand, that must determine the guidelines — and the red lines — for negotiations.

When military experts are asked, they explain that it is absolutely necessary for Israel to maintain possession of the lands taken in the Six-Day War. The reasons for this stance are plainly obvious.

---

4.  Moreover, when this course of action is followed the doctor's decision is no longer merely a medical opinion, but carries the authority of a Torah directive.

The Golan Heights command control of the entire Galilee, Israel's north. Missiles and artillery placed in the Golan could easily destroy civilian centers and military bases in the Galilee. Moreover, even in our age of hi-tech weaponry, fighting uphill is much more difficult than fighting downhill or fighting on level terrain. Thus, if Syrian troops would attack from the Golan, Israel would be put in a defensive position that would be very challenging to turn around.

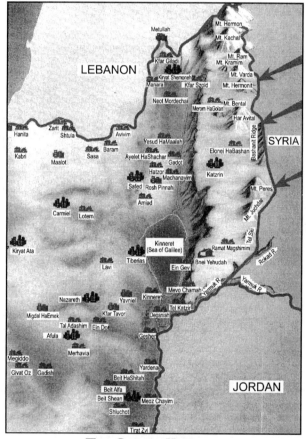

### THE GOLAN HEIGHTS
THIS RELIEF MAP SHOWS WHY THE EASTERN BORDER OF THE GOLAN
IS THE NATURAL LINE OF DEFENSE FOR ISRAEL'S NORTH

Similarly, with regard to Judea and Samaria, on the West Bank of the Jordan: these are hilly regions that overlook major Jewish coastal cities on the other side of Israel's narrow waist. An enemy army perched there could effortlessly cut Israel in half. It is not without cause that even left-leaning Israelis have called the pre-'67 borders, "the borders of Auschwitz." And even if there were no danger from an enemy army, terrorists firing rockets from those hills could paralyze the reserve call-ups on which the Israeli military depends.

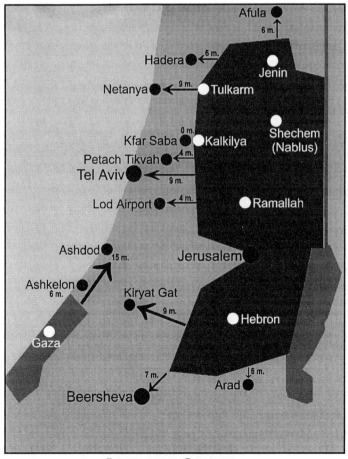

**JUDEA AND SAMARIA**
THE ARROWS INDICATE THE DISTANCES OF SOME MAJOR ISRAELI TOWNS
FROM THE BORDERS OF THE PROPOSED PALESTINIAN AUTONOMY

Although the nature of warfare has changed, strategic depth is still critical. Even in this age of missiles, the final determinant is what happens on the ground.

Witness the Gulf War. Despite weeks of bombing by planes and missiles, the Iraqis were not defeated until the land war began. Moreover, because of strategic depth, since America limited the extent of its penetration, even when his armies were defeated, Saddam Hussein's power was not shaken totally.

Maintaining possession of the lands taken in the Six-Day War is necessary not only to prevent attack, but also to protect against terrorism. There is no question that the presence of the Arab population in Judea, Samaria, and Gaza presents security problems. It is, however, far easier to control those problems when the jurisdiction over these regions is under Israeli control. First of all, life-saving intelligence about impending terrorist activity can be gathered far more easily. Secondly, preventive measures and response to terrorism can be more thorough and more efficient. Even today, before any further "redeployment" has taken place, terrorist killers simply flee to any of the nearby Cities of Refuge in the Palestinian Autonomy, secure in the knowledge that their sympathizers will grant them hospitable anonymity out of the reach of Israel's security and intelligence personnel.

For these reasons, when considering solely the security perspective, no military expert has ever counseled return of the lands Israel conquered in '67. On the contrary, military men from the US and other countries have been amazed that Israel has spoken about making any concessions.

Who have offered such concessions? Politicians, including some military experts who have become politicians.

Why are they willing to consider these concessions? — Because they feel that peace will resolve all these difficulties, that once peace is established security considerations will be unnecessary. If these people are asked what is required from a strictly security perspective, they answer that these lands should not be returned. Nevertheless, they explain that they are willing to take a risk for the sake of peace.

When questions of life and death are involved, one does not take risks based on what may or may not happen in the future. How can lives be risked because the situation will perhaps change in the future? Whose lives are being taken so lightly?

How can we know what will happen in the future? Supposing that an Arab leader would be willing to enter into a full and complete peace treaty with Israel. Should security considerations be relaxed because of such an offer?

Absolutely not. The Arab regimes are for the most part totalitarian dictatorships prone to coups and unpredictable changes of heart. What would happen if the leader who made peace fell? Would his successor keep up the agreement? In such a scenario, Israel would have compromised its security, and brought an enemy closer, without having any guarantee of her future safety.

And if this is true when complete peace is being offered, how much more so is it true at present when the Arab leaders have trouble making public offers of even a "cold" peace with Israel?

The future is always uncertain. Weaponry is becoming more sophisticated. What is a slight security risk today may become a major risk tomorrow. Jewish law states that a person should not endanger his own life — and of course, not that of others — when there is only a possibility that his actions will save the life of another person. By contrast, everything should be done to avoid the possibility of danger arising.

The Code of Jewish Law (*Shulchan Aruch, Orach Chaim* 329:6) states:

> When there is a [Jewish] city close to the border, then, even if [enemies mount an attack, although they] come only for the purpose of [taking] straw and stubble, we should [take up arms] and desecrate the Sabbath because of them. For [if we do not prevent their coming] they may conquer the city, and from there the [rest of the] land will be easy for them to conquer.

What is the law saying? That even when an enemy attack does not pose an immediate danger to life, since allowing them control of a border city puts the entire land in danger, we should take up arms to prevent that danger from arising.[5]

This is precisely the situation in Israel today. Every inch of territory in Israel is like a city on the border; it is vital for her security. Giving it away to the Arabs exposes all her inhabitants to the possibility of attack.

This is why so many Jewish leaders are saying that not one inch of land should be returned. This reason is unconnected with the holiness of the land or the fact that they love it.

Yes, the land is holy, and yes, there are people who love it, but the reason the land should not be returned is not this holiness or this love. Instead, this is a life-threatening issue; the lives of millions of our people are at stake. To sum it up:

---

5.   Significantly, this law applies not only in the Land of Israel, but also in the Diaspora. Indeed, its source (Tractate *Eruvin* 45a) gives as an example a city in Babylonia in which the Jews lived while in exile. This emphasizes that the concern at hand is not the sanctity of the Land of Israel, but rather the preservation of Jewish life.

Security provisions should never be sacrificed in order to achieve what appears as diplomatic success.

## PEACE FOR PEACE

The proposition of exchanging land for peace is unheard of in the annals of history. Whenever has a nation that won territory in a defensive war surrendered it to the very nations which attacked it?

And will giving back land lead to peace? Let us look at the situation as it is. Never in the history of Israeli-Arab relations have concessions led to an attitude of conciliation and peace. Instead, the initial concessions have communicated feelings of weakness and insecurity that have been exploited by the Arabs and have encouraged them to make further and more excessive demands. Every retreat before pressure has called forth greater pressure to retreat even further.

A pattern has been established: The Arabs make vociferous demands. Afraid of "cutting off our dialogue," we make concessions, agreeing to at least several of their claims. And shortly afterwards, they demand more, explaining to us and to the world at large that these new claims are logical corollaries to the claims that we have already accepted.

And there is a certain logic to their argument. After all, once Israel has accepted the basic premise that it is proper to compromise its security to placate the Arabs, it is hard to draw red lines. If danger to life is no longer a reason to say "No; no more," what is?

It is high time we stopped merely reacting, and establishing our policies in response to Arab claims. Instead, we have to be concerned with our own priorities. We have to know that there are certain things that are simply not for sale. They will not be presented on the bargaining table. And this restriction is not prompted by sentimental reasons; it is simply that one does not take risks when lives are at stake.

## WHEN IS PEACE MORE LIKELY?

Not only is the land for peace theory dangerous; it has no logic to it. Take for example, the Golan. Despite all the vehement anti-Israeli rhetoric emanating from Damascus since 1974, and even though Syrian troops were involved in the Lebanon War in 1982, there has never been an attack mounted from the Syrian front. Why? For a very simple reason. Situated on the Golan Heights, Israeli artillery is pointed directly at Damascus. The terrain is more or less flat, and tanks and infantry can advance without great difficulty. In such a situation, any Syrian leader will think hard before he contemplates a war with Israel. The risks are far too high.

Consider for a second the situation if that were no longer true, if there were no Israeli guns on the Golan, and Syrian guns were positioned there instead. If the deterrent of fear were removed by Israel's ceding the Golan, would the likelihood of a Syrian attack be increased or decreased?

Giving away land for peace means exchanging strategic positions for a mere piece of paper. And it is legitimate to question how much that piece of paper is worth. For the Arabs have broken every treaty they ever made with Israel. And, for that matter, they have a sorry record of keeping the agreements they have made among themselves.

## Do the Arabs Really Want Peace?

Many times in their internal propaganda, the Arabs have said that their involvement in the peace process is part of their "holy war to liberate Palestine." Sadat said it bluntly when he explained to the Arabs why he visited Jerusalem: He told them that he paid lip-service to the concept of peace because he knew that in this way he could receive more from Israel than he could ever win in a war. Afterwards, he explained, once Egypt's position was improved and Israel's was weakened, he could wage war from a position of strength.

A look at the school textbooks and news media in Egypt — a country which is officially at peace with Israel — reflects whether or not the Arabs have taken the concept of peace seriously. Their press — which is all government controlled — seethes day after day with anti-Israeli editorials and anti-Semitic caricatures. At school, in their history classes, children are taught about the imperialistic intent of the Zionist invaders. And Friday after Friday, a message of hatred resounds from the mosques.

Whoever wants a clear picture of whether or not the Arabs desire peace should ask the ordinary Arab in the street. He will respond — as has been documented by many polls — that he is not opposed to violence against Israel, and that he desires Arab dominion over the entire land of Palestine. Have we forgotten the Palestinians who danced on their roofs with glee when Iraqi Scuds fell on Israel?

Can they be blamed for such an attitude? The average Arab is certainly not responsible for these feelings. These are the values on which he has been raised for years. For him to defy them would mean challenging his society's entire hierarchy.

But absolving the ordinary Arab from blame should not lead us to ignore the situation which prevails. From the heads of state to the ordinary man in the street, the Arab world's attitude toward Israel is one of hatred and contempt; never have there been any serious attempts toward coexistence.

## WHY LET TERROR AND PEACE
## GO HAND AND HAND?

Because of this deep-seated hatred, there are many Arabs willing to engage in terrorist activity against Israel. Even were the Arab leadership to totally divorce itself from terrorist activity (something which has not yet been done), there would still be a danger of terrorist activity from individual fanatics.

Unfortunately, however, the danger of terror does not come only from the extremist fringe. Instead, the Arab leadership actively encourages terror, because terror wins concessions at the conference table.

A pattern has been established. First demands are made. Then terrorist attacks create a mood of fear and uncertainty. And afterwards, the Arab leadership clamors that the attacks are justified because of oppression and explains that the situation can be quieted by concessions. An agreement is reached and is swallowed by the Israelis.

What has happened? The Arabs have learned that through terror and through clamor they can win concessions, that the Israelis are willing to sacrifice their security bit by bit to win temporary calm.

And so the pattern continues. From time to time there is an ebb, but never a cessation. First Arab demands, then Arab terror, then escalation of the demands, and finally Israeli concessions.

To counter this trend, Israel must broadcast a clear message: Terrorism will be met with strength; when caught, terrorists and their families will be punished severely; and by no means will terrorism be rewarded by concessions.

## WHY WON'T WE SAY WHAT THE EMPEROR IS [NOT] WEARING?

Why won't the Israelis face the facts and speak about them openly? Why won't they acknowledge that from the beginning until the present all the peace process has accomplished is to strengthen the Arab position?

There are two reasons. First of all, it would jeopardize their own credibility. They risked entering into negotiations and/or agreements with the Arabs, and they feel that admitting that the Arabs have not relented, would be considered a failure. If they would say: "Look, the emperor is naked; there are no new clothes; the Arabs have not made any moves toward peace," they fear that their own garments would also look pretty shabby. They would have to admit that they had endangered the security of their land with a mistaken approach.

So what is done instead? They ignore the danger and try to camouflage it so that others will not see it as well. There were times when terrorist attacks were reported in Western news media before the official media in Israel even mentioned them. On numerous occasions, rather than expose the charade in the Arab peace effort, Israel has reinforced the Arab position by publicly recognizing them as "partners in the endeavor to reach peace."

But the Israeli difficulty with speaking honestly about the peace process goes deeper than the self-interest of the leaders who have embraced it. Israel has continually chosen to worry first about what other nations will say, and second about its own priorities. Rather than focus on what is necessary for our own security, growth and development, the attitude has always been: What will the Arabs say? And what will the response from Washington be?

Not that there is anything novel in this attitude. Over three thousand years ago, the returning scouts whom Moses had dispatched to report on the inhabitants of the Promised Land debriefed as follows:[6] "We were like grasshoppers in our own eyes, *and so we were in theirs.*" It all begins with our own self-image, how we look at ourselves. When we perceive ourselves as puny, when we cower within, it is no surprise that our enemies will act aggressively toward us. Conversely, when we have self-respect, when without boastful pride we focus on our own priorities and give precedence to our own security, other nations will regard us differently.

After the Six-Day War there was a real fear of Israel and her army within the Arab world. Today, sadly, that is no longer true. Why? Because of our concessions, because of our inability to stand up and claim what is rightfully ours, they perceive us as weak. And a weak enemy invites aggressiveness.

The same applies with regard to Israel's relations with America. If Israel will not stand up for her priorities, can one expect America to fight for them? If Israel will not protest the constant Arab violation of agreements, why should America be concerned with them?

Even when we need help from other nations, we need not cower before them in fear. America considers foreign aid as an investment. And every investor will be more impressed with a prospective partner who — though not boastful or arrogant — knows what he needs and wants and is forthright in seeking it.

---

6.   *Numbers* 13:33.

## OUR RIGHT TO THE LAND OF ISRAEL

There is a fundamental argument that must be dealt with. At the bottom of all the Arab rhetoric lies one basic claim: "You are intruders. This is our land. We had been living here for centuries and then you decided to take it from us."

Once it is established that the Jews have a valid right to the Land of Israel, then the violence, hatred, and disregard for life that has characterized the Arab position can be judged for what it is. Unless that right is established, the Arabs will always claim that they have a valid goal: reclaiming a land that is rightfully theirs. And once validity is granted to their goal, the debate whether all means are acceptable to attain it or not is one of philosophy.

What is our claim to the land? —G-d's promise in the Torah. G-d told Abraham:[7] "I have given this land to your descendants." For one-and-a- half thousand years the Land of Israel was our home, and ever since then, Jews everywhere have longed to come home to their eternal heritage — to Jerusalem, the site of the Holy Temple;[8] to Hebron, the burial place of Abraham, Isaac and Jacob;[9] and to Bethlehem, where Rachel weeps for her dispersed children and awaits their return.[10] Even throughout the two thousand years during which our people wandered from country to country, Israel has remained the national home of every Jew. From the beginning of the exile until this day, no matter how farflung his current host country might be, every Jew has turned to face the Holy Land in his thrice-daily prayers.

---

7.   *Genesis* 15:18.
8.   *I Kings*, ch. 8.
9.   *Genesis*, ch. 23.
10.  *Jeremiah* 31:14-16.

So central is this principle to our faith, that *Rashi,* the foremost of the traditional commentators on the Torah, begins his commentary by stating:

> Rabbi Yitzchak said: The Torah should have begun with the verse,[11] "This month shall be for you the first of the months...," for this introduces the first commandment given to Israel.
>
> Why then does it begin with the narrative of creation?...
>
> So that if the nations of the world say to Israel, "You are robbers, because you took by force the lands of the seven nations [of Canaan]," Israel will reply to them: "The entire world belongs to the Holy One, blessed be He; He created it and gave it to whomever He pleased. Of His own will He gave it to them, and of His own will He took it from them and gave it to us."

From this perspective the entire Land of Israel — not only the coastal region, Jerusalem, and the Galilee, but also Judea, Samaria, and indeed every tiny portion of the land — is part of an organic whole, an indivisible and sanctified unity. In this spirit, the Kneisiyah HaGedolah of Agudas Yisrael, an assembly of Jewry's foremost sages in the pre-Holocaust era, declared in 1937:

> The Holy Land, whose boundaries were prescribed by the Holy One, blessed be He, in His holy Torah, was granted to the nation of Israel, the eternal people. Any sacrifice of the Holy Land that was granted to us by G-d is of absolutely no validity.

This explanation is, moreover, the only rationale that cannot be refuted by the Arabs or the Americans. They also

---

11. *Exodus* 12:2.

accept the Bible and believe in the truth of its prophecies. The Koran does not dispute the Jews' right to the Land of Israel. And can you conceive of an American president telling his people that G-d's promise to Abraham is not relevant? Indeed, the connection between the land and our people is so well established that everywhere it is referred to as "the Land of Israel."

For this reason, it is important to emphasize that this connection is rooted in the Bible's prophecies. It would not be desirable to base our claim to the Land of Israel on the Balfour Declaration or international agreements of the present century, for these agreements could be countermanded by other ones. After all, how favorable is the United Nations to Israel today?

Nor is the fact that our people once lived in the land sufficient in and of itself to establish our claim to it today. If the American Indians would lodge a claim to all of America, would it be granted them?

When the Bible's prophecies serve as the basis for our claim, then many other arguments are effective in reinforcing the position. But when that foundation is lacking, we have difficulty refuting the gentiles' claim: "You are robbers, because you took by force the lands of the... nations."

After thousands of years of exile, our people have returned to our land. Every portion of the land over which Jewish authority is exercised was won in defensive wars in which G-d showed overt miracles. Now when G-d grants His people land in such ways, should it be returned? Is it proper to spurn a Divine gift?

## PRACTICALLY WHAT TO DO NOW

The most immediate step to solving the problem is to settle the entire land. Wherever there is open space in Judea, Samaria, Gaza, and the Golan, settlements should be established. There is no need to displace Arabs; there is ample empty land.

This should not be done with fanfare. The idea is not to create an image, but to create a reality. When the land is settled by Jews, it will become obvious to all that we consider this as Jewish land, not theoretically, but practically. Indeed, the fact that settlement is the issue which the Arabs protest most vehemently should make it clear that it is Israel's highest priority. It is the most pragmatic means at Israel's disposal to change the balance of power in her favor. Once widespread settlement becomes a fact, it will impossible to turn back the clock. The Arabs outside Israel will appreciate that the borders will not be moved back. And the Arabs inside Israel will understand that their future exists in coexistence with the Jews and not with struggle against them.

Unquestionably, there will be protests at the outset. They must be met with resolution. When this is done, the Arabs and the other nations will ultimately realize the reality: Israel is serious about defending her self-interest; this land will not be given away.

For this purpose, it is important that new settlement be broad in scope. The same clamor will be raised by the Arabs whether a new home is added to an existing settlement, one new settlement is founded, or the entire land is settled. So why hold back?

Indeed, restrictions against settlement invite protest. For it becomes obvious that restrictions are imposed only because in essence there are Israels who feel that they don't really belong there. Settling the land without restriction, by contrast, broadcasts a message of confident self-esteem. It shows the entire world that Israel is doing everything possible to maintain her security and will not be halted in that endeavor.

## WHAT AMERICA WANTS

It is hard to believe, but it is happening. The primary US interest in the Arab countries has always been oil. And yet today, when conservation programs, solar energy, and other by-products of advanced technology have reduced the world's dependence on oil, the Arab bias in American foreign policy has grown instead of being reduced.

It does not make sense. There is no question in anyone's mind that Israel is America's only reliable friend in the Middle East. No one has forgotten that less than a decade ago Arafat, Assad, and others were openly declared enemies of American policy. Their speeches are on record. All that is necessary to do is open the archives of any newspaper. Indeed, anti-American slogans are so much a part of their rhetoric that even today they occasionally voice them. And yet, in three-way negotiations, they are getting the upper hand.

So what happened? The fundamental difficulty is that Israel has not had the strength to stand up against pressure. What she has won on the battlefield, she has surrendered at the negotiating table.

It is true that America pressured Israel. But America did pressure or would have also pressured the Arabs. When an American president or negotiator sits down with Arabs and Israelis, his intent is the bottom line: that an agreement be signed. He is not so much concerned with the nature of the agreement. He assumes that each party will watch out for its own self-interest. What he is concerned with is that the parties walk out of the room having signed an agreement. And to make sure that objective is reached he will use both a carrot and a stick.

What has happened? Time and time again, the Israelis have buckled under pressure. Even when all the cards were in their hand, they have given in to Arab demands. Take, for example, the Camp David agreements: Carter needed a treaty for his election campaign. Sadat needed a treaty to put himself in the American camp. He had already burnt all his bridges behind him. Who had the strongest position? Begin. And yet he gave in to all the Arab demands.

Of course there was pressure, intense pressure. But if Begin had said "No," that same pressure would have been exerted on Sadat, and he could not have afforded to say no. Nevertheless, Begin conceded.

This did not happen only once. On the contrary, a pattern was established. When an agreement was necessary, pressure was applied on Israel, and almost inevitably, she conceded.

And so, it became almost a knee-jerk reaction in the State Department: Apply pressure to Israel; it works.

Also, the logical basis for the Israeli position became weakened, for the red lines were always being redrawn. The Americans never really knew what was really not up for negotiation.

The proof of the argument is that on several occasions, Israel has stood firm, and refused to compromise her position; for example (until the rise of the Peres government), on the status of Jerusalem. In these instances, despite the fact that there were Arab demands and American pressure, when the Arabs saw that Israel was firm and would not compromise on these issues, they were removed from the agenda.

## PROJECTING AN IMAGE

In a larger sense, the problem with the peace negotiations has never begun at the bargaining table. The Israeli disadvantage always began long beforehand. Even before sitting down together, Israel was put on the defensive.

Israel has difficulty confronting its self-image. Hard as it is to conceive, Israel has difficulty coming to terms with its identity as a Jewish state. For that reason, there is so much rhetoric against the orthodox and the observant. Because of this difficulty, Israel has never come out and said: "This is Jewish land, given to us by G-d, and necessary for our own security." Instead, it offers all sorts of arguments to try to justify its possession of the land according to "universal values."

But this does not work. The international community is solidly behind the Arabs, and even in the US, support for Israel has waned.

Why? Because Israel's self-image is confused, the external image it projects comes out distorted. Since the real truth is not being said, what is being said is being disregarded or misinterpreted.

Consider: Israel spends prodigious funds and effort for the welfare of its Arabs. Indeed, the standard of living of the Arabs in Judea and Samaria — before the Intifada — was far superior to that of the average person in most Arab countries. And yet Israel is portrayed throughout the world as a cruel, despotic, and oppressive regime. She bends over backwards to prove herself just and righteous in the eyes of the other nations, and yet continually incurs their censure.

At times, this situation borders on the ridiculous. To cite a case in point: In the midst of the Lebanon War, Lebanese Christians murdered hundreds of Palestinians at the refugee camps of Sabra and Shatilla. No Israelis were actually involved in the killings. Instead, this was a case of one Arab taking revenge against another, a time-honored tradition in the Arab world. To prevent these killings from taking place, Israeli soldiers would have had to risk their own lives.

How did Israel react to the killings? She volunteered to take the blame. "Since the Israeli soldiers did not stop the Christians, they are responsible for the deaths," so certain quarters of Israeli society argued. And so loud was their protest that a Commission of Inquiry was established, which made recommendations resulting in a shuffling of the Israeli Cabinet and Army High Command.

How was this heard throughout the world? — That Israel admitted causing the massacre of hundreds of Palestinians. Now, it is true that innocent people did not have to die. But in the world's eyes, the people who actually caused the murder were not condemned whereas the Israelis were.

There is a need for Israel to put first things first, to clarify to herself what her priorities are and to go out and put those priorities into practice. This will raise her stature in the community of nations.

Why do the other nations condemn Israel so frequently? — Because Israel is so concerned with what they say, because the conception of Israel in the world outside and not the country's own priorities determines Israeli policy. And so when you can meddle, thinks the world at large, why not meddle?

There are many nations — including several of the Arab countries so vehement in their criticism of Israel — which flagrantly violate human rights and yet they are rarely, if ever, called to account for this by the world community. The reason: These countries simply will not listen.

Israel must also learn to show strength. And in her instance, the strength can come, not from hollow bravado, but from genuine principles, foremost among them being the need to protect the lives of her citizens. And when this course of action is applied resolutely, she will win respect in the world at large.

## CONCERN THAT LEAPS
## OVER GEOGRAPHIC BOUNDARIES

Many readers will probably ask: "Of what practical concern is all this to me? There is no way that I can have an effect on Israeli policy, so why should I become involved?"

There are two responses:

(a) First of all, like or not, we are all involved. Every Jew is bound to every other Jew: a threat to a Jewish community in any part of the world affects Jews all over the world. How much more so is this true when the Land of Israel is involved. *For every Jew, wherever he lives, possesses a portion in the Land of Israel.*[12] *And the Land of Israel possesses a portion of every Jew, a piece of our heart and soul.*

When (heaven forbid) there is a war in Israel we feel involved and we do what we can to help. Today Israel is being besieged, not militarily, but diplomatically. She is suffering severer losses of territory in the conference rooms than she would ever suffer on the battlefield.

(b) To a large extent, this struggle is taking place in the public media of the Western countries and among their opinion-makers. These media portray the Arabs as an

---

12. Rabbeinu Meir ben Baruch (Maharam of Rothenburg, Responsum 536, *Otzar HaGeonim, Kiddushin,* sec. 146), rules that every Jew owns four cubits of land in the Holy Land. Accordingly, our Sages apply universally certain principles of Jewish business law that are relevant only to a person who owns real estate.

oppressed people, peacefully seeking to regain what is rightfully theirs. Lies and falsifications are repeated so frequently that they become accepted as immutable truths. And this background supports the Arabs when they sit down at the negotiating table.

This is where people in the Diaspora can make a difference — by working to set the record straight. Most cases do not call for much convincing. When a terrorist kills a mother and a child, is it difficult to make people understand that an outrage has occurred? When an Arab government ignores its own commitments, shouldn't a newspaper carry the story? Each of us can do his bit to correct Israel's image in the community and country in which he lives.

Throughout Part I of this presentation, we have tried to make several points:

(a) Saving and protecting the lives of its citizens is the foremost priority of any government, how much more so when we are speaking of a Jewish government and Jewish life. Therefore:

(b) In the Land of Israel today, security provisions should never be sacrificed in the hope of achieving diplomatic success.

(c) Concessions do not breed an attitude of conciliation and peace. Instead, they communicate a stance of weakness that is exploited by the Arabs for pressing further and more extensive demands.

(d) The Arabs have never yet taken the concept of peace seriously. Any lip-service to the ideal of peace was intended for one purpose alone: to receive whatever they can without fighting.

(e) Israel has constantly operated from an inferiority complex, trying to find favor in the eyes of the other nations, instead of placing her own security as her priority.

# PART II:

## PHASES IN THE ISRAEL-ARAB CONFLICT: ISRAELI APPROACHES & SUGGESTED ALTERNATIVES

If only the above arguments were mere abstractions to be bartered about in a political science class or philosophical discussions to be politely shared over the dinner table! Unfortunately, however, they are facts of life, truths have been largely ignored by Israeli governments over the past 30 years. As a result, a recurring pattern has been established. Concession after concession has been made to the Arabs without anything substantial being received in return. Time and again, victories won with blood and Divine miracles on the battlefield have backfired into defeats at the negotiating table. Thousands of Jewish — and for that matter Arab — lives have been lost. The term "peace process" has become virtually synonymous with demands for Israeli concessions.

Throughout this period, against this background of concessions, a different voice was heard. For decades, until 1994, the Lubavitcher Rebbe served as a rockbed of strength and confidence, radiating guidance and vision for the future of our land and its people.

This is not mere history. At present as well, the Rebbe's insights remain current and foresighted. His insights and advice shed light on how to deal with the problems we face today.

In the pages to follow, we will present a brief historical overview of several phases in the Arab-Israeli controversy and the directives and perception the Rebbe shared at the time. The intent is not merely to recount the past, but rather to point towards the future. If mistakes and adverse factors are highlighted, it is not to thrive on negativity, but to spell out problematic approaches that continue to undermine Israeli policy until the present day. Reviewing the past may prevent us from living it.

And, through rethinking the past, we can chart a path of action for the future, one that will lead to security, growth, and hopefully peace within the Land of Israel.

## THE SIX-DAY WAR AND ITS AFTERMATH

Today, it is hard to recapture the feelings that existed before the Six-Day War. At that time, people everywhere — including most of the Jewish community inside and outside Israel — sincerely believed the Arab threats to push Israel into the sea. They felt that it was only a matter of time before those threats would be carried out. As the war drew nearer and nearer, their premonitions of dread continued to increase.

The Rebbe, in contrast, radiated strength and confidence. Before the war, he made both public and private statements, stating that this was a period of unique Divine favor for the Jewish people, and promising that they would soon be rewarded by wondrous miracles. When American students in Israel were streaming to the airport by the thousands, the Rebbe told his followers to stay in the Holy Land, assuring them that they did not face any danger.

Immediately after the war was concluded, the Rebbe began to speak out against the return of the territories Israel had conquered. At that point, no one could appreciate what the Rebbe meant. Never in world history had any one ever thought of returning land won in a defensive war.

And yet, shortly after the war, a state delegation from Jerusalem arrived in Washington and told the Americans to advise the Arabs that Israel was prepared to give back the land she had conquered in exchange for peace.

At first the Americans were amazed; they did not believe what they were hearing. But when the Israelis repeated their promises, they communicated the message. The Arabs, flabbergasted, had not dreamed that Israel would ever consider giving away these territories. The Americans, however, assured them that the Israelis meant what they said.

Why didn't the Arabs agree? Because at that time, they could not contemplate giving even lip service to the concept of peace. So powerful was their hatred that they could not publicly state that they would end their aggression against Israel.

And yet, the fact that they digested the Israeli message was harmful. From that moment, they launched a diplomatic campaign calling for the return of the land that Israel had conquered. Had Israel not made these offers, the Arabs would never have contemplated making such demands.

A similar pattern could be seen with regard to the Arabs living in the West Bank. Directly after the war, the majority of the Arabs wanted to flee to the other Arab countries. Many others would have gladly done so had they been offered some financial recompense. At that point in time, the other Arab countries would have accepted them. They would have had no choice. And yet Israel's leaders closed the borders and prevented these Arabs from leaving.

At that time, Israel's government explained that they were encouraging the Arabs to stay because they wanted to show the world a shining example of coexistence between nations. What shortsightedness! Had they left, the Intifada, the demographic problem, and all the sensitive issues that a large Arab population in the West Bank creates would never have arisen. And any significant reduction in the Arab population would have diminished the magnitude of these problems.

Nor is shortsightedness the only difficulty. The greater reason for having the Arabs stay was that Israel's self-image was not strong enough to see herself settling the entire land and maintaining possession. Although from a security perspective this is vital for the country's future, the Israeli government lacked the inner resolve to make this commitment to the country's tomorrow.

Instead, the government restricted Jewish settlement in the Old City of Jerusalem and throughout the West Bank. Rather than create a situation which would have made the unity of the holy city and the continued possession of the West Bank a logical necessity, the Israeli government always treated the land as "occupied territory." Indeed, this conception was continually reinforced by government communiqués and the official government news media, which always referred to the West Bank as *hashtachim* ("the territories"), instead of the Hebrew names for Judea (Yehudah) and Samaria (Shomron). Moreover, the government always treated the Arabs as the rightful owners of the land, clearly indicating that a just settlement of the issue would involve an Israeli withdrawal.

From the outset, the Rebbe called for settlement of the entire land, emphasizing that not only from a spiritual perspective, but also from a security perspective, the Land of Israel is a single, indivisible entity. He did not see the government's program of partial settlement as a solution, for it placed the settlers in danger, and never reflected a sincere commitment to command authority over the land in its entirety.

## THE WAR OF ATTRITION

After the Six-Day War, the Arab hostilities against Israel continued. Across the entire stretch of the Suez Canal, bloody artillery battles were fought between Israeli and Egyptian troops.

At that time, the Nixon administration expended considerable effort to broker a cease-fire between the two sides. During the lengthy negotiations the Rebbe warned Israel against entering into any agreement, explaining that Egypt wanted a cease-fire only to begin preparing for the next war. "Before the ink is dry on the agreement," the Rebbe warned, "the Egyptians will violate it. And who knows how many lives will be lost in the next war because of these violations."

The Israelis had the upper hand. Their armies were at the banks of the Suez Canal and by preventing its use put a stranglehold on the Egyptian economy. Nevertheless, in the negotiations, the Egyptians made demands with bravado. At first the Israelis hesitated, but as the negotiations continued, the Israel acceded to every one of the Egyptian demands.

What was the agreement's saving grace for the Israelis? There was to be a cease fire: although the Israelis would pull back, the Egyptians solemnly promised not to move any heavy guns across the Suez.

What actually happened? *The day after the treaty was signed* the Egyptians violated it, moving their artillery and anti-aircraft batteries across the Suez and entrenching them in the Sinai Peninsula. The transfer of equipment was photographed and publicized by news media throughout the world.

What did the Israelis do? They lodged a few feeblehearted protests and then carried on as if nothing had happened. They could have launched an artillery attack that would have destroyed the Egyptian guns before they could be positioned. No one in the world could have protested, for the Egyptians had flagrantly violated the agreement before its ink had dried.

But Israel's army was silent, and even her diplomats did not voice constant and outspoken protests.

What was the rationale motivating the Israelis? First of all, the hope that the agreement would be a first step toward peace, and second, the perception that signing this treaty would win American favor and enable Israel to receive American arms.

Neither of these perceptions had any basis in reality. To imagine that Nasser could have been at all prepared for peace with Israel, one would have had to be an incorrigible dreamer. Yet when the parents of the soldiers who had been killed in the three previous years asked the government why the concessions to the Arabs were being made, this is the answer that was given them.

Nor was it necessary to make these concessions to receive American arms. America did not desire Israel's position to be weakened. Just as she expected the Arabs to make demands she expected Israel to reject them, because they were harmful to her security. How was she to know that Israel would capitulate to every single Arab demand?

What happened as a result of the Israeli redeployment mandated by the treaty? The Egyptians were able to cross the Suez without difficulty in the Yom Kippur War of 1973 and their anti-aircraft batteries in the Sinai inflicted losses on Israeli planes. Although the treaty did give the Israelis a temporary respite from battle, in the long run it cost many more lives.

And most importantly, had Egypt not been given these strategic positions, it is very possible that the Yom Kippur War would never have been waged. It was only because Egypt had been granted a foothold in the Sinai that she had the position and the confidence to launch an attack.

## THE YOM KIPPUR WAR

In the months leading to Yom Kippur, 1973, Israeli intelligence had gathered reports of an Arab troop build-up and the possibility of war. To combat such forces, they warned, Israel was not able rely on her standing army, and had to call up her reserves. Nevertheless, each time the Prime Minister and the cabinet were alerted, the warnings were rejected. "There is no need," explained Golda Meir, "to sow panic among the populace."

In the days before the war, and even on the day the war broke out, the cabinet met, and the nation's military leaders demanded that the reserves be called up, for the Arabs were obviously preparing for war. They explained that the call-up itself might prevent the war. For if the Arabs saw that Israel was ready, they might hesitate before launching an attack. At the very least, the call-up would place the Israelis in a position to repulse the attack, and launch an immediate counterattack.

Despite the army's urgent insistence, the cabinet remained unwilling. In her autobiography, Golda Meir admits that she and her advisors had intelligence reports of an impending attack. Nevertheless, they refrained from calling up the reserves so that the world would see that Israel was not an aggressor. Allowing herself to be attacked would clearly demonstrate Israel's peaceful intent to the Americans and encourage them to support her with arms.

The argument is so absurd that it is difficult to write it down in a manner which makes any sense at all, but that is what happened. Because of the government's desire that Israel appear as a peace-loving nation, a fierce war which cost over two-and-a-half thousand Jewish lives ensued. A large proportion of those casualties took place in the first days, when Israel's lack of preparation left her open to Arab attack. And because of the Arab advances during those first days, Israel was forced to fight from compromised positions later on.

Nor was this the end of the Israeli willingness to sacrifice her security because of what a few politicians imagined international opinion to be. When the Israeli army succeeded in turning the tables and launching a counterattack against Syria and Egypt, they met immediate success. They reconquered large portions of the Golan and proceeded toward Damascus. Although they were only short miles away from the Syrian capital, and there was no substantial opposition in front of them, they suddenly halted their advance. Instead of conquering the Syrian capital, the Israeli army simply sat still.

Because they did not advance, the Syrians had time to regroup their artillery, and inflict losses on the Israelis. But that was not the most severe loss the Israelis suffered. The war ended shortly afterwards. Had Damascus been conquered, Syria would have been defused as a power for decades. Instead, after the war, she emerged as Israeli's most belligerent foe.

Why didn't Israel seize this opportunity? Because her diplomats overruled her generals. The diplomats were afraid of world opinion. But whose opinion? Not that of the Communist bloc. They had sided with the Arabs and could never be won to the Israeli side. The Americans? They would have been overjoyed if Syria was conquered. Syria had openly identified with the Russians, and America wanted nothing more than to have her power restricted.

True, at the outset, America would have protested. In order to appease the Arabs, it would have had to make a gesture. But everyone would have realized that it was merely a gesture. Israel could have gone about dealing with her own security needs without any interference.

True, such a campaign would have caused losses. But there have been Israeli losses on the Syrian front ever since. And the danger of greater losses still persists. When a person has a malignant disease he does what is necessary to deal with the problem. An operation may be painful, but it is preferable to allowing the malignancy to spread. The faster action is taken the better.

A similar mistake was made on the Egyptian front. Egypt's Third Army had penetrated the Sinai Desert, but there they were surrounded by Israeli troops. Their supply line was cut and they were without food and water. The vanguard of the Israeli troops had already crossed the Suez, and were threatening the Egyptian capital. Not surprisingly, the Egyptians began to sue for a cease fire. Although they had started the war, they now wanted to end it as soon as possible.

Did Israel demand the surrender of the Third Army? No. They allowed the Egyptians to receive humanitarian aid from relief organizations. As a result, because they had not surrendered, it was recognized in the cease-fire agreement that this army had recaptured portions of the Sinai. A brilliant turnover on the battleground was again soured into a defeat by the diplomats at the negotiating table.

Why? Because they were unwilling to stand firm, and wait for the pressure to be placed on Egypt. At that point, the Egyptians needed the cease fire more than the Israelis, and yet in their desire to appear as peace-loving, Israel made concession after concession.

In New York, the months preceding the war were also charged by intense activity. Although he was not privy to the intelligence information coming out of Israel, the Rebbe began a campaign to strengthen Jewish education for children. Citing the verse,[1] "Out of the mouths of babes and sucklings You have established the strength... to destroy an enemy and an avenger," the Rebbe explained that the Torah study of young children generates protective spiritual influences for the Jewish people. For months, the Rebbe repeated and expounded this verse at public gathering after public gathering, in letters, and in personal meetings. He later stated that he had felt impelled from above to take this step.

After the war broke out, at public gatherings and at private meetings with Israeli leaders, the Rebbe spoke out fiercely against Israel's unwillingness to conquer Damascus. "When I asked army commanders why they didn't conquer Damascus," the Rebbe said, "they told me that it is surrounded by rocky terrain which makes an advance difficult. Had I not heard this myself, I would not have believed that such an excuse could be given."

Over and over again, the Rebbe urged Israelis to recognize that they had been saved by a Divine miracle: instead of proceeding further after breaking through the Bar-Lev line in the Sinai and Israel's initial defenses on the Golan, the Egyptian and Syrian troops had halted their advance. That halt had given Israel the time to mobilize her reserves. With thankful acknowledgement, the Rebbe continued, Israelis should have wisely used the advantage provided to them by the new territories they had conquered and not sacrificed them because of the whims of several diplomats.

---

1.   *Psalms* 8:3.

## COURAGE AND FORTITUDE, BUT WHOSE? —
## THE CAMP DAVID ACCORDS

In 1977, one man captured the attention of the entire world, bringing about a change in the paradigm of Israeli-Arab relations. Anwar Sadat decided to visit Israel.

Until that time, Israeli and Arabs had seen each other face to face only on the battlefield, and now they would talk to each other directly without intermediaries.

Sadat had courage. Realizing that the path of action that he and his predecessors had been following had not brought him success, he was concerned about his country's future. Something new had to be done. So instead of listening to the worn-out tapes of advice he had received from Egyptian advisors, from other Arab leaders, from Washington and from Moscow, he decided to do something different, something which no one had ever dreamed of. He would go to Israel.

What was his intent? He wanted the return of the territory Egypt had lost in the Sinai; he wanted the time to rebuild his army without the threat of war; and he wanted American financial aid for his country.

Did he genuinely want peace with Israel? We can never know. To the other Arab leaders, he explained that he was not surrendering anything. He would receive what he could without fighting. And then, having improved Egypt's position, he said, he would leave the challenge of defeating Israel militarily to the next generation.

Was there nothing more? Were all the overtures of peace merely for show? Again, we cannot know. Twenty years later, the reality is that Israel's sacrifice of its dearly-developed oilfields almost destroyed its economy. There is a very cold peace between Egypt and Israel. There is next to no economic cooperation. At every international diplomatic or commercial event in Egypt, Israel's representatives are demonstratively snubbed. Egyptian tourists almost never come to Israel. In Egyptian media and schools, Israel is still described as "the enemy." The Egyptian army is stockpiling arms, and from time to time, Egyptian leaders speak of war against Israel.

But was that Sadat's intent? Had he have lived, would it have been different? Firstly, that itself is a lesson — that when making a treaty with an enemy, one has to take the worst possible scenario in mind, not merely hope for the best. We can never know what will happen in the future, and we cannot make real sacrifices in the mere hope that everything will work out.

Secondly, for peace to have been achieved, the bold ability to step beyond paradigms which Sadat demonstrated would have had to have been countered by a similar approach on the Israeli side, and unfortunately, that was lacking.

Peace can never be achieved when only one side gives and the other merely receives. This does not nurture an attitude of respect for an adversary. On the contrary, weakness encourages an adversary to try to take greater advantage. When both sides have surrendered something, there is a chance that they will consider an agreement worth honoring, but when one side has made all the sacrifices, the other side has nothing binding it. And that is what happened at Camp David.

Before Camp David, Israel controlled strategic mountain passes that would have made an Egyptian troop advance difficult; she had airfields in the Sinai which gave her advantages in both defensive and offensive movement; and she had oilfields which guaranteed her energy supply in time of war and supported her economy in peace. All these she sacrificed. In addition Begin gave the order to bulldoze the beautiful seaside township of Yamit, together with its surrounding cluster of thriving agricultural settlements on the Israeli side of the Gaza Strip.

In return Israel was handed a piece of paper; Sadat gave nothing of substance.

But the fault in the Israeli approach goes deeper. Sadat became a hero in Israel. He was lauded all over the country, and celebrations were held for his arrival. Israelis were overjoyed that an Arab leader had actually acknowledged their existence. So great was the adulation that there were Knesset members who proposed making Arabic a required language in schools.

Now did any such thing ever happen in Egypt? Or, for that matter, did American praise ever wax so eloquent when a Russian leader came to visit? It seemed that Israel was saying, "Well, since Sadat thinks we're important, I guess we are." Self-esteem came not from an inner sense of their own mission and purpose, but from the recognition granted by a foe.

Sadat heard that message, and for that reason he made no concession.

Israel spoke to him as if he was the leader of all the Arab countries. In particular, she made commitments to him with regard to the West Bank. It was at Camp David that the term "autonomy" was coined.

The Palestinians had stated publicly that they did not see Sadat as their representative. He had no commitment to them, nor they to him. For sure, to try to upgrade his image in the Arab countries he felt it necessary to raise the Palestinian issue. But once it was raised, Israel could and should have answered the truth: "This is no concern of yours. Peace with the Palestinians has to be made with the Palestinians." And he would have left it at that, for his interests really lay only in strengthening his own country.

Nevertheless, the Israelis made commitments to him, acknowledging a limitation of their rights to the West Bank.

For him, making the requests was almost a caprice. He had nothing to lose, so why not ask? But the Israelis had everything to lose, and nothing to gain by speaking to him about the issue. And yet they spoke — and made concessions.

In general, there was no reason for Israeli concessions. Sadat needed American support and money and could not get that without signing a peace treaty with Israel. He had already burned his bridges with the other Arab countries, and would not restore his image by breaking off negotiations with Israel and coming back emptyhanded. Carter was deeply involved in a reelection campaign and needed an agreement to improve his prestige among the voters.

Begin, by contrast, needed nothing. There was nothing substantial that Sadat was prepared to give, and within Israel, the fact that he was the prime minister who had brought Sadat to Jerusalem had bolstered his position immensely. Unquestionably, Sadat was going to make demands, and the Americans may have supported him initially, but Begin held all these cards in his hand; there was no reason for him to give in. And yet he made concession after concession, giving away (and even volunteering) security and economic assets without getting anything in return. This was unnecessary. He could have come away with a treaty without making any substantial concessions.

Is this mere conjecture? Not at all, because on one of the most sensitive points of all the negotiations, Begin stood his ground, and Sadat conceded. Sadat had demanded that Begin make concessions with regard to Jerusalem. On this point Begin stood firm and said, "No."

Now Jerusalem has sentimental value to the Arabs. A pledge from Begin on an altered status for Jerusalem would have been very flattering to Sadat's image. But when Begin stood firm, the matter was erased from the agenda.

The same motif could have been followed with regard to other matters. Sadat could have made demands, but Begin could have said "no." If he had said "no" firmly, the American pressure that had been placed on him would have shifted to Sadat. And Sadat would have had to concede, for he had more to lose. Indeed, from the time of Sadat's visit onward — significantly, many of the points mentioned above were made by the Rebbe in a public address delivered on the very night Sadat landed in Israel — the Rebbe argued that fortitude and patience were the only path to true peace.

Throughout the entire time, the Rebbe raised a cry of protest against the Israeli approach. Indeed, Camp David marks the beginning of the fifteen years during which the Rebbe repeatedly warned that the proposed autonomy would quickly grow into an armed and belligerent Palestinian state which would displace Israel and destroy the basic security of her Jewish inhabitants.

When Egypt violated the agreements, putting far more military men in the Sinai than the treaty allowed, the Rebbe called for a halt to the Israeli implementation of the remaining clauses. "Why continue withdrawing from land when the Egyptians are not maintaining their commitments?" he repeatedly asked. "Why the stubbornness on the part of the Israelis to observe every minor detail of the agreement, when the Arabs, those who have benefited most from it, violate the few restrictions which they undertook to honor?"

## Lebanon

In 1982, after the residents of the Upper Galilee had been forced to spend night after night in bomb shelters out of fear of Katyusha rockets, the Israeli army invaded Lebanon with the intent of rooting out the PLO terrorist bases there.

At the outset, the campaign met with almost miraculous success. One enemy position after another fell until the Israelis had surrounded the PLO headquarters in East Beirut. The majority of the leaders of the terrorist groups who had attacked Israel for years could have been captured and the backbone of the terrorist organizations broken.

And then Israel stopped. They could have cut off food, water, and electricity; they could have reduced the city to rubble. But they didn't. Instead of demanding unconditional surrender, they let the terrorists leave — taking their weapons with them.

No war is desirable. But if an unavoidable war has been undertaken, if casualties have been suffered, and total victory is in sight, it is ludicrous not to seize it.

What prevented Israel from seeking total victory? First of all, criticism at home. Lebanon was Israel's Vietnam. Israel was forced to fight with one hand tied behind her back because of cries for peace from its own populace.

Had they not entered into a war, one might have debated whether it was justified. But they had entered a war; they had already suffered casualties, and the enemies they were fighting were not humanitarians, but terrorists who had killed women and children.

Our Sages teach:[2] "Whoever is merciful to the cruel, will ultimately be cruel to the merciful." The misplaced mercy

---

2.   *Yalkut Shimoni* on *Samuel*, sec. 121.

during the time of the war in Lebanon has been responsible for the death of hundreds of Israelis in the years that followed.

The second reason for holding back was fear of US pressure. Once again Israel repeated the errors of the Yom Kippur War. It seems almost too simple to say: No nation sacrifices its soldiers and its critical objectives because of possible censure from other nations. Surgeons do not stop operations in the middle.

Moreover, the Israelis misjudged the intent of the Americans. The US had no love for the PLO. Particularly, at that time, Cold War tensions were high and the PLO were identified with Russia. Moreover, they were terrorists who had attacked Americans. If one looked at America's genuine interest, it was clearly to back Israel.

It is true that America may have made some protests to Israel. But they were not accompanied by threats. Indeed, President Reagan undertook a diplomatic mission to Europe for nine days, granting Israel time to complete unfinished business. While on the road he would have had ample reasons to explain why he had done nothing to restrain the Israelis. And shortly afterwards, Secretary of State Haig resigned, giving Israel more time to use while the State Department changed hands. Nothing would have happened if Israel had gone about taking care of her own priorities, and made her explanations afterwards.

Not only was this not done. As mentioned above, Israel was her own worst enemy, taking blame for atrocities when there was no need or justification for her to do so. And for her pathetic attempts at proving her humanitarian intent, she was rewarded with censure after censure.

The most painful aspect of the war was the months — and years — of limbo when Israel had halted its actions against the terrorists, but kept its army in Lebanon. Why did the soldiers remain? Because the government realized that the objectives of the war had not been achieved. And yet, too afraid to actually achieve those objectives, they left their soldiers in enemy territory, sitting ducks for terrorist attacks. Life after life was sacrificed on the altar of indecision as a government hamstrung by fear of what the world would say ruminated about the steps it should take.

Months before the war the Rebbe called in several of Israel's leading chassidim and directed them to begin writing a Torah scroll, each letter of which would be inscribed for a particular Israeli soldier who had sponsored it. This the Rebbe did as a means to promote the safety and security of the Israeli army in general and of every participating soldier in particular.

Throughout the war the Rebbe was outspoken in his criticism of the Israeli government for its vacillation and hesitation, for its willingness to sacrifice the lives of its soldiers and citizens in order to humor the whims of world opinion. Above all, the Rebbe pointed his finger at the root of the problem: the unwillingness of Israelis to look in the mirror and identify their own security as their foremost concern.

## AUTONOMY AND INTIFADA

In 1989, there began a series of riots and strikes in Arab villages and cities in the West Bank. The Israeli government responded with equivocation. Instead of using controlled and directed force to stop the protests, it allowed the Arabs to continue violent and provocative activity. Cars of Jewish motorists passing through the West Bank were stoned by the thousand. The government's response: Buy shatterproof windshields.

As the unrest in the West Bank was allowed to fester, there was an increase in international demands that Palestinian rights be respected. At this time, a cycle began which has continued until the present day. Unrest and violent activity on the West Bank is used to create international pressure on Israel to make concessions; these concessions, in turn, spur greater unrest and violent activity, which evoke even greater concessions.

Matters reached the point at which, in an attempt to save face, the Israelis would simply not report terrorist activities, unless and until they were forced to do so by the prior publicity of Western media. To this day, nowhere in the Western media — or for that matter in the Israeli media — is the danger that exists for Israeli cars traveling in Judea and Samaria properly documented.

The same is true of the precarious security predicament of Jewish settlers even now, when the autonomy extends to only a limited number of regions in the West bank. As the autonomy expands, the Jewish settlements within its territory are becoming vulnerable islands surrounded on all sides by hostile armed forces. In a sudden mass attack (which in Eastern Europe used to be called a pogrom) just before Purim, 1996, in the yeshivah building at the Tomb of Joseph in Shechem (Nablus), fifteen soldiers were killed and sixty other Jews were wounded — by arms which Israel had handed to the Palestinian Autonomy's "police force" as part of the "peace process"....

Several times during the Intifada, the Rebbe made public and private statements citing the counter-productive effects of the Israeli policy. Speaking with obvious pain, the Rebbe stated clearly that concessions would increase terrorist activity, rather than discourage it. "The concessions convince the Arabs of Israeli weakness," he emphasized. "They make it clear that terrorism is effective in achieving results. Even mere talk of possible concessions is harmful because it encourages terrorist activity."

"You understand Arabic," the Rebbe told one of the Israeli cabinet ministers who visited him. "Ask the Arab in the street. See what *he* thinks will be the end result of the peace process."

On the same occasion, im 1992, after the Rebbe had exerted the full weight of his influence to bring about the election of Shamir, he declared that he would oppose Shamir's regime with equal vigor — because in the meantime Shamir had changed his tune, resuming where Begin had left off.

## THE GULF WAR

In 1990, almost six months before the Hebrew year 5751 began, the Rebbe declared that the Hebrew letters indicating the numerical equivalent of the coming year also formed an acronym for the Hebrew phrase meaning, "This will be a year when I [G-d] will show them [the Jewish people] wonders."[3]

Before the previous year, the Rebbe had foretold that it would be "a year of miracles," and indeed that year was marked by the collapse of the Iron Curtain and the emigration of hundreds of thousands of Soviet Jews to our Holy Land. And yet, the Rebbe assured his listeners, the wonders of 5751 would surpass those of 5750.

While the Rebbe was delivering this message, preparing the Jewish people and the world at large for these developments, urgent preparations of a different kind were being made in a distant corner of the world. In August of 1990, Saddam Hussein marched the armies of Iraq into Kuwait, plunging the entire world into panic. As heads of government, opinion-

---

3.   Cf. *Micah* 7:15.

makers in the media, and ordinary men and women in the street reacted in fear, the Rebbe spread a message of quiet optimism.

In Israel, gas masks were handed out in fear of chemical warfare and thousands fled from the land in dread of Iraqi missiles. So complete was the fright that when Yasser Arafat stood together with Saddam Hussein and offered an Iraqi pullback in return for a Palestinian state, there were Israelis who urged acquiescence.

The Rebbe, by contrast, reassured the world that chemical weapons would not be used in Israel. He publicly referred to Israel as "the safest place in the world," and urged Americans to travel there. When Major J. Goldstein, a chaplain dispatched by the US army to the war zone, asked about the projected length of the hostilities, the Rebbe assured him that the war would be over by the festival of Purim (which, as is widely known, is exactly when hostilities ceased).

There is no need to recount the entire saga of how the Rebbe's vision was vindicated. It is sufficient to point to the repeated expressions of thanks given by Prime Minister Shamir for the strength and confidence which the Rebbe imparted to people throughout Israel.

## WHAT THE FUTURE HAS IN STORE

Israel is at a turning point in its history. If the path of previous governments is to be followed, it will find itself making concession after concession until the Arabs will have established themselves confidently enough to wage war.

There is an alternative: to stop, to retrench; to realize that Israel has the potential to develop a creative society, one which is strong internally, and which has the vitality to endure the challenges posed by its neighbors; to look to the guidelines of the Rebbe outlined above.

Are we condemned to perpetual war? First of all, we must look ourselves squarely in the face and say, "Perhaps." For the answer to that question does not depend on ourselves alone. We did not start any of the previous wars. They were all started by belligerent foes who surround us and are still bent on our destruction. This is a reality which we must honestly face rather than blindly hope for peace.

Moreover, accepting that reality makes peace a more practical option. When the Arabs know that Israel will not continue to concede, and that she will not fight wars with her hands tied behind her back, they will begin to genuinely understand how serious the option of war is. And this will hopefully lead to peace.

Take a look at the Cold War: Militarily, it was a standoff. Each side had enough arms to deter the other from attack. The lines were drawn, and fear protected one side from the other. Then one day it was over. The totalitarian backwardness that characterized Russian society could not stand up to the challenge of the times, and the Kremlin collapsed. America, by contrast, had a strong and vital society which was able to adjust.

Similarly, in the case at hand, when the Arabs realize that Israel is strong, and is not making further concessions, they will have to come to terms with the situation. If they choose war, at least Israel will be able to defend itself from a position of strength.

Most likely, however, that position of strength will make war less of an option. Unless Israel continues to compromise its security, no Arab country will dare to attack it. Consider: Why didn't Jordan enter the Yom Kippur War? Why didn't

Syria open up a second front on the Golan in the Lebanon War? This choice did not stem from any great love for Israel. It was a practical decision. Their capitals were too close to the front to take the risk.

And when there is a military détente, there is a chance that the socio-economics of a world economy that is pressing toward the ideal of a global village will make the Arabs consider peace as an option. Today, all the world's leading countries are turning towards peace, not because they have become more refined and peaceloving, but simply because it is in their self-interest. The benefits of peace and the costs of war outweigh any possible gains that could be achieved on the battlefields. As Israel and the Arab countries become involved in this motif, it will affect them as well.

Similar concepts apply with regard to the Palestinian problem. The Palestinians are tired of losing their sons and their daughters; they are frustrated by the fact that they haven't been able to work freely and advance themselves financially for the last decade. When they recognize Israel's firmness, and understand the limits of what they can possibly achieve through the Intifada, they will focus their attention on their own lives and the options that are open to them.

These are real possibilities. When Israel decides to take its future in its hands, and with faith and trust in G-d, focuses on strengthening its security and building a strong and viable society, it will be able to face the future confidently. The miraculous half-century of growth that has followed the Holocaust can be followed by even greater advances. And hopefully, these advances will include the dawning of the age in which "nation will not lift up sword against nation, nor will they learn war any more."[4]

---

4.   Isaiah 2:4.

# PUBLICATIONS AVAILABLE FROM
# SICHOS IN ENGLISH—5757/1997

- ❑ Letters to N'Shei Chabad ............................................................ $5.00
- ❑ Basi LeGani .............................................................................. $7.00
- ❑ On Ahavas Yisroel—Heichaltzu ................................................. $14.00
- ❑ Likkutei Dibburim Vol. II ............................................................ $17.00
- ❑ Likkutei Dibburim Vol. III ........................................................... $17.00
- ❑ The Chassidic Dimension Vol. 1 ................................................ $17.00
- ❑ The Chassidic Dimension Vol. 2 ................................................ $17.00
- ❑ The Chassidic Dimension Vol. 3 ................................................ $17.00
- ❑ Sefer HaMinhagim .................................................................... $17.00
- ❑ The Shabbat Primer .................................................................. $9.00
- ❑ The Nechoma Greisman Anthology ........................................... $15.00
- ❑ With Light and With Might ........................................................ $7.95
- ❑ To Know G-d—Veyadaata ........................................................ $7.95
- ❑ Timeless Patterns in Time Vol. 1 ............................................... $17.00
- ❑ Timeless Patterns in Time Vol. 2 ............................................... $17.00
- ❑ To Know and To Care .............................................................. $17.00
- ❑ Please Tell Me What The Rebbe Said Vol. 1 .............................. $12.95
- ❑ Please Tell Me What The Rebbe Said Vol. 2 .............................. $12.95
- ❑ In the Paths of Our Fathers ...................................................... $17.00
- ❑ At Our Rebbes' Seder Table (Hard Cover) ............................... $13.95
- ❑ At Our Rebbes' Seder Table (Soft Cover) ................................. $8.95
- ❑ In the Garden of Torah Vol. I .................................................... $17.00
- ❑ In the Garden of Torah Vol. II ................................................... $17.00
- ❑ The Ladder Up ......................................................................... $12.00
- ❑ A Partner in the Dynamic of Creation ...................................... $15.95
- ❑ Proceeding Together Vol. I ....................................................... $17.00
- ❑ Proceeding Together Vol. II ...................................................... $17.00
- ❑ The Chassidic Approach to Joy ............................................... $14.00
- ❑ Beautiful Within ....................................................................... $5.00
- ❑ The Making of Chassidim ......................................................... $17.00
- ❑ Links in the Chassidic Legacy .................................................. $18.00
- ❑ Defiance and Devotion ............................................................ $14.00
- ❑ The Curtain Parted Vol. I .......................................................... $14.00
- ❑ Likkutei Sichos—Bereishis—Vol. VI .......................................... $16.00
- ❑ Likkutei Sichos—Shemos—Vol. VII .......................................... $16.00
- ❑ Likkutei Sichos—Vayikra—Vol. VIII .......................................... $16.00
- ❑ Vedibarta Bam—Bogomilsky—Bereishit ................................... $16.00
- ❑ Vedibarta Bam—Bogomilsky—Shemot ..................................... $16.00
- ❑ Vedibarta Bam—Bogomilsky—Vayikra ..................................... $16.00
- ❑ מגולה לגאולה (Hebrew) .............................................................. $17.00
- ❑ From Exile to Redemption Volume I ........................................... $17.00
- ❑ From Exile to Redemption Volume II .......................................... $17.00
- ❑ As A New Day Breaks ............................................................... $15.00
- ❑ Mashiach—Schochet ............................................................... $7.00
- ❑ המשיח (Hebrew)—Schochet ..................................................... $7.00
- ❑ Highlights of Mashiach—Stone ................................................. $3.50
- ❑ Sound the Great Shofar ........................................................... $14.00
- ❑ תקע בשופר גדול (Hebrew) .......................................................... $10.00
- ❑ Seek Out the Welfare of Jerusalem .......................................... $17.00

❏ Anticipating the Redemption ....................................................$14.00
❏ Let's Get Ready (children) ...........................................................$7.50
❏ To Live and Live Again.................................................................$17.00
❏ Nechama/Mendel Get Ready for Moshiach ...........................$9.95
❏ Sichos In English Vol. 17 Nissan—Elul, 5743 ..............................$10.00
❏ Sichos In English Vol. 20 Adar II—Iyar, 5744.............................$10.00
❏ Sichos In English Vol. 22 Tammuz—Elul, 5744.............................$10.00
❏ Sichos In English Vol. 23 Tishrei—MarCheshvan, 5745..............$10.00
❏ Sichos In English Vol. 24 MarCheshvan—Shevat, 5745............$10.00
❏ Sichos In English Vol. 25 Shevat—Nissan, 5745.........................$10.00
❏ Sichos In English Vol. 26 Nissan—Sivan, 5745 ...........................$10.00
❏ Sichos In English Vol. 27 Tammuz—Elul, 5745 ...........................$10.00
❏ Sichos In English Vol. 28 Tishrei—MarCheshvan, 5746..............$10.00
❏ Sichos In English Vol. 29 MarCheshvan—Shevat, 5746...........$10.00
❏ Sichos In English Vol. 30 Shevat—Nissan, 5746.........................$10.00
❏ Sichos In English Vol. 31 Iyar—Tammuz, 5746............................$10.00
❏ Sichos In English Vol. 32 Tammuz—Elul, 5746 ...........................$10.00
❏ Sichos In English Vol. 33 Tishrei—Kislev, 5747 ...........................$10.00
❏ Sichos In English Vol. 34 Kislev—Adar, 5747 .............................$10.00
❏ Sichos In English Vol. 35 Adar—Sivan, 5747..............................$10.00
❏ Sichos In English Vol. 36 Tammuz—Elul, 5747 ...........................$10.00
❏ Sichos In English Vol. 41 Adar I—Sivan, 5749.............................$10.00
❏ Sichos In English Vol. 42 Tammuz—Elul, 5749 ...........................$10.00
❏ Sichos In English Vol. 43 Tishrei—Teves, 5750............................$10.00
❏ Sichos In English Vol. 44 Teves—Iyar, 5750 ...............................$10.00
❏ Sichos In English Vol. 45 Iyar—Elul, 5750 ..................................$10.00
❏ Sichos In English Vol. 46 Tishrei—Teves, 5751 ...........................$10.00
❏ Sichos In English Vol. 47 Teves—Nissan, 5751 ..........................$10.00
❏ Sichos In English Vol. 48 Nissan—Sivan, 5751 ...........................$10.00
❏ Sichos In English Vol. 49 Tammuz—Elul, 5751 ...........................$10.00
❏ Sichos In English Vol. 50 Tishrei—Kislev, 5752 ...........................$10.00
❏ Sichos In English Vol. 51 Kislev—Adar, 5752 .............................$10.00

## TAPES

❏ #1—Relationship Between G-d & Creation ............................$20.00
❏ #2—Chassidic Approach to Attain Joy....................................$20.00
❏ #3—The Spiritual Dimension of Mitzvos...................................$20.00
❏ #4—The Spiritual Realm..............................................................$20.00
❏ #5—The Animal Soul and the G-dly Soul................................$20.00
❏ #6—The Different Kinds of Souls ...............................................$20.00
❏ #7—The Concept of the "Rebbe".............................................$20.00
❏ Yechidus: Chosid-Rebbe Relationship ....................................$20.00
❏ Hol. 1—Rosh Hashana, Yom Kippur, Sukkos...........................$20.00
❏ Hol. 2—Simchas Torah, Chanukah, Purim ..............................$20.00
❏ Hol. 3—Passover & Days of the Omer .....................................$20.00
❏ Hol. 4—Shavuos, Tisha B'Av, Month of Elul.............................$20.00
❏ Mashiach Set 1 .............................................................................$20.00
❏ Mashiach Set 1 .............................................................................$20.00
❏ Mashiach Set 1 .............................................................................$20.00
❏ History of Rebbeim of Chabad Set 1.........................................$20.00
❏ History of Rebbeim of Chabad Set 2.........................................$20.00
❏ History of Rebbeim of Chabad Set 3..........................................$20.00

מוקדש

לחיזוק ההתקשרות לנשיאנו

כ״ק אדמו״ר זי״ע

◆

נדפס ע״י
הרה״ת ר׳ **יוסף יצחק הכהן** וזוגתו מרת **שטערנא מרים**

בניהם ובנותיהם
**שרה רבקה** ובעלה הרה״ת **שמעי׳**
ובנותיהם **ריזל** וחי׳ **מושקא** שיחיו **קרינסקי**
**מרדכי זאב הכהן, זלמן שמעון הכהן,**
**חי׳ שצערא, איסר אשר הכהן, זהבה, חנה,**
**ישראל הכהן, רפאל הכהן וריזל**
שיחיו לאורך ימים ושנים טובות

**גוטניק**